WILD ANIMALS

MUSK OXEN

BY ABBY DOTY

WWW.APEXEDITIONS.COM

Copyright © 2026 by Apex Editions, Mendota Heights, MN 55120. All rights reserved. No part of this book may be reproduced or utilized in any form or by any means without written permission from the publisher.

Apex is distributed by North Star Editions:
sales@northstareditions.com | 888-417-0195

Produced for Apex by Red Line Editorial.

Photographs ©: Shutterstock Images, cover, 1, 4–5, 6, 7, 8–9, 14–15, 16–17, 18–19, 20–21, 22–23, 24–25, 26, 27, 29; iStockphoto, 10–11, 12–13

Library of Congress Control Number: 2025930913

ISBN
979-8-89250-550-5 (hardcover)
979-8-89250-586-4 (paperback)
979-8-89250-654-0 (ebook pdf)
979-8-89250-622-9 (hosted ebook)

Printed in the United States of America
Mankato, MN
082025

NOTE TO PARENTS AND EDUCATORS

Apex books are designed to build literacy skills in striving readers. Exciting, high-interest content attracts and holds readers' attention. The text is carefully leveled to allow students to achieve success quickly. Additional features, such as bolded glossary words for difficult terms, help build comprehension.

TABLE OF CONTENTS

CHAPTER 1
CIRCLE UP 4

CHAPTER 2
BIG BODIES 10

CHAPTER 3
HUGE HERDS 16

CHAPTER 4
LIFE CYCLE 22

COMPREHENSION QUESTIONS • 28
GLOSSARY • 30
TO LEARN MORE • 31
ABOUT THE AUTHOR • 31
INDEX • 32

CHAPTER 1

CIRCLE UP

A herd of musk oxen searches for food. Suddenly, the oxen hear howls nearby. A pack of wolves runs toward the group.

Musk oxen often rush to higher ground when in danger.

The musk oxen move together. They form a large circle. Young calves rush to the middle. The wolves growl outside the circle. They nip at the oxen.

At the outside of a circle, bigger musk oxen point their horns toward attackers.

Arctic wolves can run 46 miles per hour (74 km/h).

STAY AND FIGHT

Wolves are much faster than musk oxen. So, oxen cannot run away. They must stay and fight. The weakest oxen stay safe in the middle of the circle.

Musk oxen have sharp horns. They can be deadly to other animals.

A huge ox charges. Its horns hook on to a wolf. The ox throws the attacker away. The other wolves run off, too. The herd is safe.

FAST FACT
A musk ox's horns never stop growing. Some are 24 inches (60 cm) long.

9

CHAPTER 2

BIG BODIES

Musk oxen are huge **mammals**. Males can reach more than 800 pounds (360 kg). All musk oxen have **stocky** bodies and short legs.

Wide hooves help musk oxen dig and move through snow.

A musk ox has two layers of fur. The inner layer traps warm air near the body. The outer layer keeps out the snow and cold.

OLD OXEN

Long ago, ice covered much of Earth. Many animals went **extinct**. But musk oxen survived. Their thick fur helped them stay warm.

A musk ox sheds its inner coat in spring. It grows back in fall.

Musk oxen live in the **Arctic**. They can be found in the **tundra** of Alaska and Canada. Oxen also live in Norway and Russia.

FAST FACT
Musk oxen can survive in temperatures below −40 degrees Fahrenheit (−40°C).

In the cold Arctic, plants may grow for only a few months each year.

CHAPTER 3

HUGE HERDS

Musk oxen live in herds. Most herds have 20 to 40 oxen. Usually, herds grow during winter. Oxen can stay close together for warmth.

Large herds can include up to 75 musk oxen.

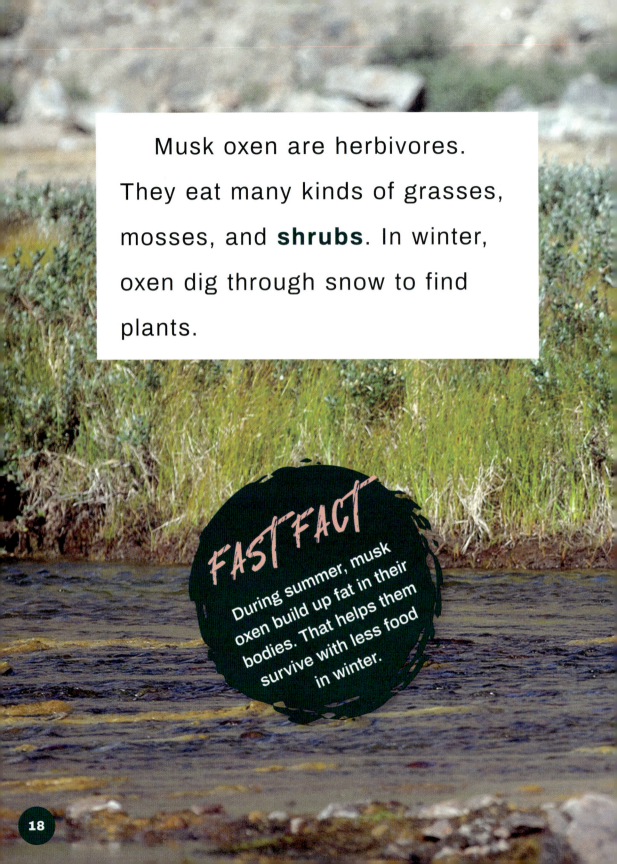

Musk oxen are herbivores. They eat many kinds of grasses, mosses, and **shrubs**. In winter, oxen dig through snow to find plants.

FAST FACT

During summer, musk oxen build up fat in their bodies. That helps them survive with less food in winter.

Many musk oxen live near rivers during summer.

19

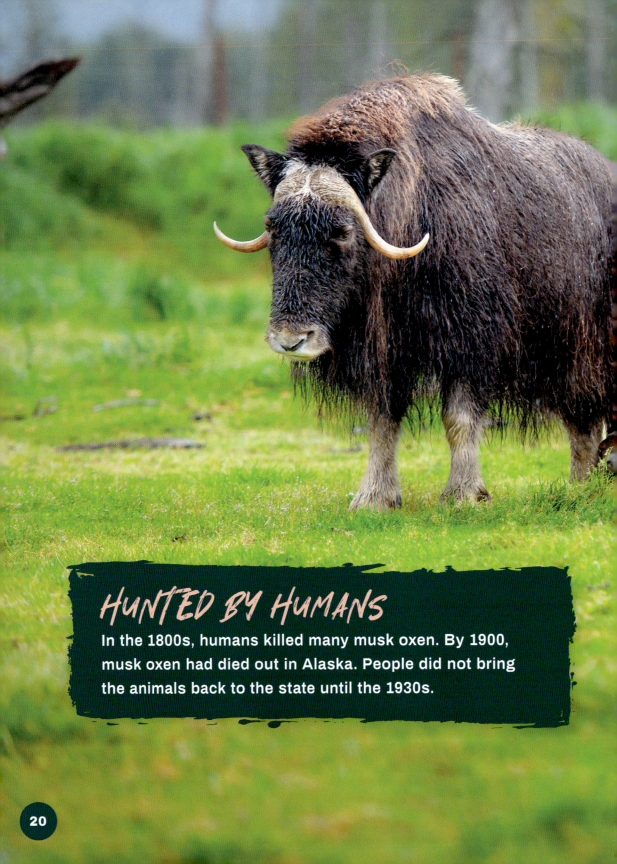

Hunted by Humans

In the 1800s, humans killed many musk oxen. By 1900, musk oxen had died out in Alaska. People did not bring the animals back to the state until the 1930s.

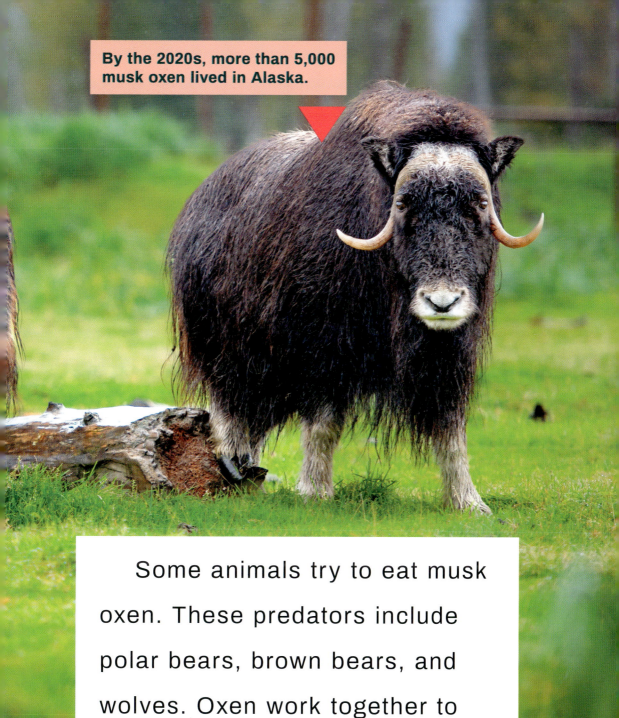

By the 2020s, more than 5,000 musk oxen lived in Alaska.

Some animals try to eat musk oxen. These predators include polar bears, brown bears, and wolves. Oxen work together to keep attackers away.

CHAPTER 4

LIFE CYCLE

Musk oxen **mate** in summer and fall. A male ox's body creates a strong smell during this time. The smell **attracts** females.

Musk oxen were named after their strong smell. The word *musk* means "a powerful, long-lasting scent."

Male musk oxen charge up to 35 miles per hour (56 km/h) when fighting.

Male musk oxen may fight over females. They charge at one another and butt heads. The winning males can mate with the herd's females.

FAST FACT

Male musk oxen's horns form bands over their foreheads. That protects their brains.

Newborn calves weigh 20 to 24 pounds (9 to 11 kg). They grow quickly.

A female musk ox gives birth to one calf in spring. She feeds the calf milk. And she keeps the calf warm during winter. Mothers care for calves for about two years.

KEEPING UP

Newborn calves can stand and walk within hours. Within weeks, calves also start eating plants. The young oxen must keep up with the herd right away.

Musk oxen live 12 to 20 years in the wild.

COMPREHENSION QUESTIONS

Write your answers on a separate piece of paper.

1. Write a few sentences explaining the main ideas of Chapter 4.

2. What fact about musk oxen do you find most interesting? Why?

3. How long can the horns of a musk ox grow?
   - A. 24 inches (60 cm)
   - B. 40 inches (100 cm)
   - C. 800 inches (2,000 cm)

4. For how long were there no musk oxen in Alaska?
   - A. less than two years
   - B. at least 30 years
   - C. thousands of years

5. What does **herbivores** mean in this book?

*Musk oxen are **herbivores**. They eat many kinds of grasses, mosses, and shrubs.*

    A. animals that eat only plants
    B. animals that eat only meat
    C. animals that eat only in winter

6. What does **predators** mean in this book?

*Some animals try to eat musk oxen. These **predators** include polar bears, brown bears, and wolves.*

    A. animals that make their own food
    B. animals that do not need to eat
    C. animals that hunt other animals for food

Answer key on page 32.

GLOSSARY

Arctic
An area in the far northern part of the world that is very cold.

attracts
Makes something come closer.

extinct
No longer living on Earth.

mammals
Animals that have hair and produce milk for their young.

mate
To form a pair and come together to have babies.

shrubs
Bushes and other short plants.

stocky
Wide and sturdy.

tundra
An area in the Arctic with few trees and where part of the ground is always frozen.

BOOKS

Kirkman, Marissa. *Coldest Climates*. Apex Editions, 2024.
Murray, Julie. *Musk Oxen*. Abdo Publishing, 2023.
Nargi, Lela. *Tundra Biomes*. Jump!, 2023.

ONLINE RESOURCES

Visit **www.apexeditions.com** to find links and resources related to this title.

ABOUT THE AUTHOR

Abby Doty is a writer, editor, and booklover from Minnesota.

INDEX

A
Alaska, 14, 20
Arctic, 14

C
calves, 6, 26–27
charging, 9, 25
circle, 6–7

F
food, 4, 18
fur, 12

H
herbivores, 18
herds, 4, 9, 16, 25, 27
horns, 9, 25

M
mammals, 10
mating, 22, 25

P
predators, 21

T
tundra, 14

W
winter, 16, 18, 26
wolves, 4, 6–7, 9, 21

ANSWER KEY:
1. Answers will vary; 2. Answers will vary; 3. A; 4. B; 5. A; 6. C